40 Jam Recipes for Home

By: Kelly Johnson

Table of Contents

- Strawberry Jam
- Blueberry Lemon Jam
- Raspberry Peach Jam
- Blackberry Vanilla Jam
- Mango Habanero Jam
- Cherry Almond Jam
- Pineapple Jalapeño Jam
- Fig and Balsamic Jam
- Apricot Ginger Jam
- Peach Bourbon Jam
- Cranberry Orange Jam
- Plum Cardamom Jam
- Apple Cinnamon Jam
- Pear and Rosemary Jam
- Kiwi Lime Jam
- Mixed Berry Jam
- Lemon Lavender Jam
- Grapefruit Mint Jam
- Orange Marmalade
- Cantaloupe and Vanilla Jam
- Caramel Apple Jam
- Honey Plum Jam
- Pomegranate Raspberry Jam
- Peach Lavender Jam
- Blueberry Basil Jam
- Cherry Port Wine Jam
- Watermelon Mint Jam
- Guava Passionfruit Jam
- Pumpkin Spice Jam
- Rhubarb Ginger Jam
- Banana Jam
- Cucumber Dill Jam
- Tomato Basil Jam
- Elderberry Orange Jam
- Chocolate Raspberry Jam

- Lemon Thyme Jam
- Kiwi Strawberry Jam
- Vanilla Peach Jam
- Minted Melon Jam
- Gingerbread Apple Jam

Strawberry Jam

Ingredients:

- 2 pounds fresh strawberries, hulled and halved
- 4 cups granulated sugar
- 1/4 cup fresh lemon juice

Instructions:

In a large mixing bowl, combine the halved strawberries and sugar. Stir well, ensuring the strawberries are evenly coated. Let the mixture sit for about 1-2 hours, allowing the sugar to macerate the strawberries.
Transfer the strawberry and sugar mixture to a large, heavy-bottomed saucepan. Add fresh lemon juice and stir to combine.
Over medium heat, bring the strawberry mixture to a boil. Once boiling, reduce the heat to low and let it simmer. Skim off any foam that rises to the surface.
Continue simmering the jam, stirring frequently, until it reaches the desired consistency. This usually takes about 30-40 minutes.
To check the jam's consistency, place a small amount on a chilled plate. Run your finger through the jam, and if it wrinkles and holds its shape, it's ready.
Remove the saucepan from heat and let the jam cool for a few minutes.
Ladle the strawberry jam into sterilized jars, leaving about 1/4-inch headspace.
Wipe the jar rims with a clean, damp cloth to remove any residue.
Place sterilized lids on the jars and tighten the bands. Process the jars in a water bath for long-term storage or store them in the refrigerator for short-term use.

Enjoy your delicious homemade strawberry jam on toast, pancakes, or as a delightful topping for desserts!

Blueberry Lemon Jam

Ingredients:

- 4 cups fresh blueberries
- 2 cups granulated sugar
- Zest of 2 lemons
- Juice of 2 lemons

Instructions:

In a large bowl, combine the fresh blueberries and granulated sugar. Toss the berries until they are well coated with sugar. Let the mixture sit for about 1 hour to allow the berries to macerate.

Transfer the macerated blueberries to a large, heavy-bottomed saucepan. Add the lemon zest and lemon juice, stirring well to combine.

Place the saucepan over medium heat and bring the blueberry mixture to a gentle boil. Reduce the heat to low and let it simmer, stirring occasionally.

Continue simmering the jam until it thickens, usually around 20-25 minutes. To test for doneness, place a small amount on a chilled plate. If it wrinkles when you push it with your finger, it's ready.

Remove the saucepan from heat and let the blueberry lemon jam cool for a few minutes.

Spoon the jam into sterilized jars, leaving a 1/4-inch headspace. Wipe the jar rims with a clean, damp cloth to ensure a proper seal.

Seal the jars with sterilized lids and tighten the bands. Process the jars in a water bath for long-term storage or store them in the refrigerator for short-term use.

Spread this delightful blueberry lemon jam on toast, scones, or use it as a topping for yogurt or desserts. Enjoy the burst of sweet and tangy flavors!

Raspberry Peach Jam

Ingredients:

- 3 cups fresh raspberries
- 3 cups peeled and diced peaches
- 4 cups granulated sugar
- 1/4 cup fresh lemon juice

Instructions:

In a large mixing bowl, combine the raspberries, diced peaches, and granulated sugar. Gently stir until the fruit is well coated with sugar. Allow the mixture to sit for about 1 hour to let the flavors meld.

Transfer the fruit and sugar mixture to a large, heavy-bottomed saucepan. Add fresh lemon juice and stir to combine.

Over medium heat, bring the raspberry peach mixture to a boil. Once boiling, reduce the heat to low and let it simmer, stirring occasionally.

Simmer the jam until it thickens, usually around 25-30 minutes. To test the jam's consistency, place a small amount on a chilled plate. If it forms a gel-like consistency, it's ready.

Remove the saucepan from heat and let the raspberry peach jam cool for a few minutes. Spoon the jam into sterilized jars, leaving a 1/4-inch headspace. Wipe the jar rims with a clean, damp cloth to ensure a proper seal.

Seal the jars with sterilized lids and tighten the bands. Process the jars in a water bath for long-term storage or store them in the refrigerator for short-term use.

Spread this delightful raspberry peach jam on toast, muffins, or use it to enhance the flavor of desserts and pastries. Enjoy the sweet combination of raspberries and peaches!

Blackberry Vanilla Jam

Ingredients:

- 5 cups fresh blackberries
- 4 cups granulated sugar
- 1 vanilla bean, split and seeds scraped (or 2 teaspoons pure vanilla extract)

Instructions:

> In a large mixing bowl, combine the fresh blackberries and granulated sugar. Gently toss the berries until evenly coated, and let the mixture sit for about 1 hour to allow the sugar to macerate the berries.
> Transfer the blackberry and sugar mixture to a large, heavy-bottomed saucepan. Add the scraped vanilla seeds and the split vanilla bean (if using vanilla extract, add it later in the process).
> Over medium heat, bring the blackberry mixture to a boil. Once boiling, reduce the heat to low and let it simmer, stirring occasionally.
> Simmer the jam until it thickens, usually around 20-25 minutes. If using vanilla extract, add it at this point and stir well.
> To test for doneness, place a small amount of the jam on a chilled plate. If it forms a gel-like consistency and wrinkles when touched, it's ready.
> Remove the saucepan from heat and let the blackberry vanilla jam cool for a few minutes. Remove the vanilla bean if used.
> Spoon the jam into sterilized jars, leaving a 1/4-inch headspace. Wipe the jar rims with a clean, damp cloth to ensure a proper seal.
> Seal the jars with sterilized lids and tighten the bands. Process the jars in a water bath for long-term storage or store them in the refrigerator for short-term use.

Spread this aromatic blackberry vanilla jam on toast, English muffins, or use it as a topping for desserts. Enjoy the rich, fruity flavor with a hint of vanilla!

Mango Habanero Jam

Ingredients:

- 4 cups ripe mango, peeled and diced
- 1 cup habanero peppers, seeds removed and finely chopped
- 4 cups granulated sugar
- 1/2 cup apple cider vinegar
- 1/4 cup lime juice
- 1 tablespoon grated fresh ginger
- 1/2 teaspoon salt

Instructions:

> In a large, heavy-bottomed saucepan, combine the diced mango, chopped habanero peppers, granulated sugar, apple cider vinegar, lime juice, grated ginger, and salt.
> Place the saucepan over medium heat, stirring to dissolve the sugar. Bring the mixture to a boil, then reduce the heat to low.
> Simmer the jam, stirring occasionally, until the mangoes and habaneros have softened, and the mixture has thickened. This usually takes about 25-30 minutes.
> While simmering, use a spoon to skim off any foam that rises to the surface.
> Taste the jam and adjust the sweetness or spiciness according to your preference by adding more sugar or habanero if needed.
> Once the jam reaches the desired consistency (thickened but still spreadable), remove the saucepan from heat.
> Allow the mango habanero jam to cool for a few minutes before transferring it into sterilized jars, leaving about 1/4-inch headspace.
> Wipe the jar rims with a clean, damp cloth to ensure a proper seal. Place sterilized lids on the jars and tighten the bands.
> Process the jars in a water bath for long-term storage, or refrigerate for short-term use.

Spread this sweet and spicy mango habanero jam on crackers, use it as a glaze for meats, or enjoy it with cheese. Be cautious with the heat level, as habaneros can be very spicy!

Cherry Almond Jam

Ingredients:

- 4 cups fresh or frozen cherries, pitted and halved
- 2 cups granulated sugar
- 1/4 cup lemon juice
- 1/2 cup chopped almonds
- 1 teaspoon almond extract

Instructions:

> In a large mixing bowl, combine the pitted and halved cherries with the granulated sugar. Stir well and let the mixture sit for about 1 hour, allowing the cherries to release their juices.
> Transfer the cherry mixture to a large, heavy-bottomed saucepan. Add lemon juice and bring the mixture to a gentle boil over medium heat, stirring frequently. Reduce the heat to low and let the cherries simmer until they become soft and the mixture thickens, usually around 20-25 minutes.
> While simmering, toast the chopped almonds in a dry skillet over medium heat until golden brown. Stir them into the cherry mixture.
> Continue simmering until the jam reaches the desired consistency. To test, place a small amount on a chilled plate. If it forms a gel-like consistency, it's ready.
> Remove the saucepan from heat and stir in the almond extract. Let the cherry almond jam cool for a few minutes.
> Spoon the jam into sterilized jars, leaving about 1/4-inch headspace. Wipe the jar rims with a clean, damp cloth.
> Seal the jars with sterilized lids and tighten the bands. Process the jars in a water bath for long-term storage or store them in the refrigerator for short-term use.

Spread this delightful cherry almond jam on toast, use it as a filling for pastries, or enjoy it with cheese. The combination of sweet cherries and nutty almonds creates a deliciously unique flavor!

Pineapple Jalapeño Jam

Ingredients:

- 4 cups fresh pineapple, finely chopped
- 1 cup jalapeño peppers, seeds and membranes removed, finely chopped
- 3 cups granulated sugar
- 1/2 cup apple cider vinegar
- 1/4 cup lime juice
- 1 teaspoon grated fresh ginger

Instructions:

In a large, heavy-bottomed saucepan, combine the finely chopped pineapple, finely chopped jalapeños, granulated sugar, apple cider vinegar, lime juice, and grated ginger. Place the saucepan over medium heat, stirring to dissolve the sugar. Bring the mixture to a boil, then reduce the heat to low.

Simmer the jam, stirring occasionally, until the pineapple and jalapeños have softened, and the mixture has thickened. This usually takes about 25-30 minutes.

While simmering, skim off any foam that rises to the surface.

Taste the jam and adjust the sweetness or spiciness according to your preference by adding more sugar or jalapeño if needed.

Once the jam reaches the desired consistency (thickened but still spreadable), remove the saucepan from heat.

Allow the pineapple jalapeño jam to cool for a few minutes before transferring it into sterilized jars, leaving about 1/4-inch headspace.

Wipe the jar rims with a clean, damp cloth to ensure a proper seal. Place sterilized lids on the jars and tighten the bands.

Process the jars in a water bath for long-term storage, or refrigerate for short-term use.

Spread this sweet and spicy pineapple jalapeño jam on grilled meats, use it as a glaze for chicken or pork, or enjoy it as a unique topping for crackers and cheese. The tropical sweetness combined with a hint of heat creates a deliciously versatile jam!

Fig and Balsamic Jam

Ingredients:

- 2 pounds fresh figs, stemmed and quartered
- 1 1/2 cups granulated sugar
- 1/2 cup brown sugar
- 1 cup balsamic vinegar
- 1 teaspoon lemon zest
- 1 tablespoon lemon juice

Instructions:

In a large, heavy-bottomed saucepan, combine the quartered figs, granulated sugar, brown sugar, balsamic vinegar, lemon zest, and lemon juice.

Place the saucepan over medium heat, stirring to dissolve the sugar. Bring the mixture to a boil, then reduce the heat to low.

Simmer the jam, stirring occasionally, until the figs have softened, and the mixture has thickened. This usually takes about 30-35 minutes.

While simmering, skim off any foam that rises to the surface.

Taste the jam and adjust the sweetness or tartness according to your preference by adding more sugar or balsamic vinegar if needed.

Once the jam reaches the desired consistency (thickened but still spreadable), remove the saucepan from heat.

Allow the fig and balsamic jam to cool for a few minutes before transferring it into sterilized jars, leaving about 1/4-inch headspace.

Wipe the jar rims with a clean, damp cloth to ensure a proper seal. Place sterilized lids on the jars and tighten the bands.

Process the jars in a water bath for long-term storage, or refrigerate for short-term use.

Spread this rich and flavorful fig and balsamic jam on toast, use it as a condiment for cheese and charcuterie boards, or add a dollop to roasted meats. The combination of sweet figs and tangy balsamic creates a sophisticated and delicious jam!

Apricot Ginger Jam

Ingredients:

- 2 pounds ripe apricots, pitted and chopped
- 2 cups granulated sugar
- 1/4 cup fresh lemon juice
- 2 tablespoons fresh ginger, finely grated

Instructions:

In a large, heavy-bottomed saucepan, combine the chopped apricots, granulated sugar, fresh lemon juice, and finely grated ginger.

Place the saucepan over medium heat, stirring to dissolve the sugar. Bring the mixture to a boil, then reduce the heat to low.

Simmer the jam, stirring occasionally, until the apricots have softened, and the mixture has thickened. This usually takes about 20-25 minutes.

While simmering, skim off any foam that rises to the surface.

Taste the jam and adjust the sweetness or ginger flavor according to your preference by adding more sugar or ginger if needed.

Once the jam reaches the desired consistency (thickened but still spreadable), remove the saucepan from heat.

Allow the apricot ginger jam to cool for a few minutes before transferring it into sterilized jars, leaving about 1/4-inch headspace.

Wipe the jar rims with a clean, damp cloth to ensure a proper seal. Place sterilized lids on the jars and tighten the bands.

Process the jars in a water bath for long-term storage, or refrigerate for short-term use.

Spread this delightful apricot ginger jam on warm scones, toast, or use it as a glaze for poultry. The combination of sweet apricots and zesty ginger creates a wonderful balance of flavors!

Peach Bourbon Jam

Ingredients:

- 4 cups ripe peaches, peeled and finely chopped
- 2 cups granulated sugar
- 1/4 cup fresh lemon juice
- 1/4 cup bourbon whiskey

Instructions:

In a large, heavy-bottomed saucepan, combine the finely chopped peaches, granulated sugar, fresh lemon juice, and bourbon whiskey.

Place the saucepan over medium heat, stirring to dissolve the sugar. Bring the mixture to a boil, then reduce the heat to low.

Simmer the jam, stirring occasionally, until the peaches have softened, and the mixture has thickened. This usually takes about 25-30 minutes.

While simmering, skim off any foam that rises to the surface.

Taste the jam and adjust the sweetness or bourbon flavor according to your preference by adding more sugar or bourbon if needed.

Once the jam reaches the desired consistency (thickened but still spreadable), remove the saucepan from heat.

Allow the peach bourbon jam to cool for a few minutes before transferring it into sterilized jars, leaving about 1/4-inch headspace.

Wipe the jar rims with a clean, damp cloth to ensure a proper seal. Place sterilized lids on the jars and tighten the bands.

Process the jars in a water bath for long-term storage, or refrigerate for short-term use.

Spread this delightful peach bourbon jam on biscuits, toast, or use it as a glaze for grilled meats.

The addition of bourbon brings a rich and complex flavor to the sweet peaches!

Cranberry Orange Jam

Ingredients:

- 3 cups fresh cranberries
- 2 large oranges, zest and juice
- 2 cups granulated sugar
- 1/2 teaspoon ground cinnamon

Instructions:

In a food processor, pulse the fresh cranberries until coarsely chopped. Transfer them to a large, heavy-bottomed saucepan.

Add the zest and juice of the oranges to the saucepan with the chopped cranberries.

Stir in the granulated sugar and ground cinnamon, combining all the ingredients well.

Place the saucepan over medium heat, bringing the mixture to a boil. Once boiling, reduce the heat to low.

Simmer the jam, stirring occasionally, until the cranberries have softened, and the mixture has thickened. This usually takes about 20-25 minutes.

While simmering, skim off any foam that rises to the surface.

Taste the jam and adjust the sweetness or cinnamon flavor according to your preference by adding more sugar or cinnamon if needed.

Once the jam reaches the desired consistency (thickened but still spreadable), remove the saucepan from heat.

Allow the cranberry orange jam to cool for a few minutes before transferring it into sterilized jars, leaving about 1/4-inch headspace.

Wipe the jar rims with a clean, damp cloth to ensure a proper seal. Place sterilized lids on the jars and tighten the bands.

Process the jars in a water bath for long-term storage, or refrigerate for short-term use.

Spread this festive cranberry orange jam on toast, muffins, or use it as a delightful condiment for holiday meals. The combination of tart cranberries and citrusy oranges creates a perfect balance of flavors!

Plum Cardamom Jam

Ingredients:

- 4 cups ripe plums, pitted and chopped
- 2 cups granulated sugar
- 1/4 cup fresh lemon juice

- 1 teaspoon ground cardamom

Instructions:

In a large, heavy-bottomed saucepan, combine the chopped plums, granulated sugar, fresh lemon juice, and ground cardamom.

Place the saucepan over medium heat, stirring to dissolve the sugar. Bring the mixture to a boil, then reduce the heat to low.

Simmer the jam, stirring occasionally, until the plums have softened, and the mixture has thickened. This usually takes about 25-30 minutes.

While simmering, skim off any foam that rises to the surface.

Taste the jam and adjust the sweetness or cardamom flavor according to your preference by adding more sugar or cardamom if needed.

Once the jam reaches the desired consistency (thickened but still spreadable), remove the saucepan from heat.

Allow the plum cardamom jam to cool for a few minutes before transferring it into sterilized jars, leaving about 1/4-inch headspace.

Wipe the jar rims with a clean, damp cloth to ensure a proper seal. Place sterilized lids on the jars and tighten the bands.

Process the jars in a water bath for long-term storage, or refrigerate for short-term use.

Spread this aromatic plum cardamom jam on warm bread, scones, or use it as a flavorful addition to desserts and pastries. The combination of sweet plums and fragrant cardamom creates a unique and delicious jam!

Apple Cinnamon Jam

Ingredients:

- 5 cups apples, peeled, cored, and finely chopped
- 2 cups granulated sugar
- 1/2 cup brown sugar
- 1/4 cup fresh lemon juice
- 2 teaspoons ground cinnamon
- 1/4 teaspoon ground nutmeg

Instructions:

> In a large, heavy-bottomed saucepan, combine the finely chopped apples, granulated sugar, brown sugar, fresh lemon juice, ground cinnamon, and ground nutmeg.
> Place the saucepan over medium heat, stirring to dissolve the sugar. Bring the mixture to a boil, then reduce the heat to low.
> Simmer the jam, stirring occasionally, until the apples have softened, and the mixture has thickened. This usually takes about 25-30 minutes.
> While simmering, skim off any foam that rises to the surface.
> Taste the jam and adjust the sweetness or spice level according to your preference by adding more sugar or spices if needed.
> Once the jam reaches the desired consistency (thickened but still spreadable), remove the saucepan from heat.
> Allow the apple cinnamon jam to cool for a few minutes before transferring it into sterilized jars, leaving about 1/4-inch headspace.
> Wipe the jar rims with a clean, damp cloth to ensure a proper seal. Place sterilized lids on the jars and tighten the bands.
> Process the jars in a water bath for long-term storage, or refrigerate for short-term use.

Spread this delightful apple cinnamon jam on toast, pancakes, or use it as a filling for pastries. The combination of sweet apples and warm cinnamon creates a comforting and delicious jam!

Pear and Rosemary Jam

Ingredients:

- 4 cups ripe pears, peeled, cored, and finely chopped
- 2 cups granulated sugar
- 1/4 cup fresh lemon juice
- 2 tablespoons fresh rosemary, finely chopped

Instructions:

In a large, heavy-bottomed saucepan, combine the finely chopped pears, granulated sugar, fresh lemon juice, and finely chopped rosemary.

Place the saucepan over medium heat, stirring to dissolve the sugar. Bring the mixture to a boil, then reduce the heat to low.

Simmer the jam, stirring occasionally, until the pears have softened, and the mixture has thickened. This usually takes about 25-30 minutes.

While simmering, skim off any foam that rises to the surface.

Taste the jam and adjust the sweetness or rosemary flavor according to your preference by adding more sugar or rosemary if needed.

Once the jam reaches the desired consistency (thickened but still spreadable), remove the saucepan from heat.

Allow the pear and rosemary jam to cool for a few minutes before transferring it into sterilized jars, leaving about 1/4-inch headspace.

Wipe the jar rims with a clean, damp cloth to ensure a proper seal. Place sterilized lids on the jars and tighten the bands.

Process the jars in a water bath for long-term storage, or refrigerate for short-term use.

Spread this fragrant pear and rosemary jam on crackers, pair it with cheese, or use it as a unique topping for desserts. The combination of sweet pears and aromatic rosemary creates a delicious and sophisticated flavor!

Kiwi Lime Jam

Ingredients:

- 4 cups ripe kiwi, peeled and chopped
- 1 cup granulated sugar
- Zest of 2 limes
- Juice of 4 limes

Instructions:

In a large, heavy-bottomed saucepan, combine the chopped kiwi, granulated sugar, lime zest, and lime juice.

Place the saucepan over medium heat, stirring to dissolve the sugar. Bring the mixture to a boil, then reduce the heat to low.

Simmer the jam, stirring occasionally, until the kiwi has softened, and the mixture has thickened. This usually takes about 20-25 minutes.

While simmering, skim off any foam that rises to the surface.

Taste the jam and adjust the sweetness or tartness according to your preference by adding more sugar or lime juice if needed.

Once the jam reaches the desired consistency (thickened but still spreadable), remove the saucepan from heat.

Allow the kiwi lime jam to cool for a few minutes before transferring it into sterilized jars, leaving about 1/4-inch headspace.

Wipe the jar rims with a clean, damp cloth to ensure a proper seal. Place sterilized lids on the jars and tighten the bands.

Process the jars in a water bath for long-term storage, or refrigerate for short-term use.

Spread this vibrant kiwi lime jam on toast, muffins, or use it as a topping for yogurt or desserts.

The combination of sweet kiwi and zesty lime creates a refreshing and tropical flavor!

Mixed Berry Jam

Ingredients:

- 2 cups strawberries, hulled and halved
- 1 cup blueberries
- 1 cup raspberries
- 1 cup blackberries
- 3 cups granulated sugar
- 1/4 cup fresh lemon juice

Instructions:

> In a large mixing bowl, combine the strawberries, blueberries, raspberries, and blackberries. Toss the berries until they are well mixed.
> Transfer the mixed berries to a large, heavy-bottomed saucepan. Add the granulated sugar and fresh lemon juice. Stir well to combine.
> Place the saucepan over medium heat, stirring to dissolve the sugar. Bring the mixture to a boil, then reduce the heat to low.
> Simmer the jam, stirring occasionally, until the berries have softened, and the mixture has thickened. This usually takes about 25-30 minutes.
> While simmering, skim off any foam that rises to the surface.
> Taste the jam and adjust the sweetness or tartness according to your preference by adding more sugar or lemon juice if needed.
> Once the jam reaches the desired consistency (thickened but still spreadable), remove the saucepan from heat.
> Allow the mixed berry jam to cool for a few minutes before transferring it into sterilized jars, leaving about 1/4-inch headspace.
> Wipe the jar rims with a clean, damp cloth to ensure a proper seal. Place sterilized lids on the jars and tighten the bands.
> Process the jars in a water bath for long-term storage, or refrigerate for short-term use.

Spread this delightful mixed berry jam on toast, pancakes, or use it as a versatile topping for desserts. The combination of different berries creates a burst of flavors in every bite!

Lemon Lavender Jam

Ingredients:

- 4 cups fresh lemon juice and zest (from about 8-10 lemons)
- 3 cups granulated sugar
- 2 tablespoons culinary lavender buds

Instructions:

In a large, heavy-bottomed saucepan, combine the fresh lemon juice, lemon zest, and granulated sugar.
Place the saucepan over medium heat, stirring to dissolve the sugar. Bring the mixture to a boil, then reduce the heat to low.
Add the culinary lavender buds to the saucepan, stirring to evenly distribute them in the mixture.
Simmer the jam, stirring occasionally, until the lemon mixture has thickened. This usually takes about 20-25 minutes.
While simmering, skim off any foam that rises to the surface.
Taste the jam and adjust the sweetness or lavender flavor according to your preference by adding more sugar or lavender if needed.
Once the jam reaches the desired consistency (thickened but still spreadable), remove the saucepan from heat.
Allow the lemon lavender jam to cool for a few minutes before transferring it into sterilized jars, leaving about 1/4-inch headspace.
Wipe the jar rims with a clean, damp cloth to ensure a proper seal. Place sterilized lids on the jars and tighten the bands.
Process the jars in a water bath for long-term storage, or refrigerate for short-term use.

Spread this fragrant lemon lavender jam on scones, toast, or use it as a unique addition to desserts. The combination of zesty lemon and aromatic lavender creates a delightful and sophisticated flavor!

Grapefruit Mint Jam

Ingredients:

- 4 cups fresh grapefruit segments, peeled and chopped
- 2 cups granulated sugar
- 1/4 cup fresh lemon juice
- 2 tablespoons fresh mint, finely chopped

Instructions:

In a large, heavy-bottomed saucepan, combine the chopped grapefruit segments, granulated sugar, fresh lemon juice, and finely chopped mint.

Place the saucepan over medium heat, stirring to dissolve the sugar. Bring the mixture to a boil, then reduce the heat to low.

Simmer the jam, stirring occasionally, until the grapefruit has softened, and the mixture has thickened. This usually takes about 20-25 minutes.

While simmering, skim off any foam that rises to the surface.

Taste the jam and adjust the sweetness or mint flavor according to your preference by adding more sugar or mint if needed.

Once the jam reaches the desired consistency (thickened but still spreadable), remove the saucepan from heat.

Allow the grapefruit mint jam to cool for a few minutes before transferring it into sterilized jars, leaving about 1/4-inch headspace.

Wipe the jar rims with a clean, damp cloth to ensure a proper seal. Place sterilized lids on the jars and tighten the bands.

Process the jars in a water bath for long-term storage, or refrigerate for short-term use.

Spread this refreshing grapefruit mint jam on toast, use it as a topping for yogurt, or pair it with cheese and crackers. The combination of citrusy grapefruit and cool mint creates a delightful and invigorating flavor!

Orange Marmalade

Ingredients:

- 4 large oranges
- 1 lemon
- 6 cups water
- 6 cups granulated sugar

Instructions:

Wash the oranges and lemon thoroughly. Cut them in half and juice them. Set aside the juice.

Remove the pulp from the oranges and lemon, saving the seeds. Place the pulp in a cheesecloth or muslin bag and tie it securely.

Slice the orange and lemon peels into thin strips or desired thickness. If you prefer a less bitter marmalade, you can blanch the peels in boiling water for a few minutes and then drain.

In a large, heavy-bottomed pot, combine the orange and lemon peels, juice, water, and the bag of reserved pulp. Bring the mixture to a boil, then reduce the heat to low and simmer for about 1 to 1.5 hours, or until the peels are soft.

Remove the bag of pulp and allow it to cool. Squeeze any remaining juice from the bag back into the pot.

Add the granulated sugar to the pot, stirring until the sugar dissolves. Bring the mixture to a rapid boil, stirring frequently. Cook until the marmalade reaches the desired consistency, usually around 20-30 minutes.

To test for doneness, place a small amount of the marmalade on a chilled plate. If it forms a gel-like consistency and wrinkles when touched, it's ready.

Remove the pot from heat and let the marmalade cool for a few minutes.

Ladle the hot marmalade into sterilized jars, leaving about 1/4-inch headspace. Wipe the jar rims with a clean, damp cloth.

Seal the jars with sterilized lids and tighten the bands. Process the jars in a water bath for long-term storage or store them in the refrigerator for short-term use.

Spread this classic orange marmalade on toast or use it as a delightful accompaniment to scones and pastries. Enjoy the bright and citrusy flavor!

Cantaloupe and Vanilla Jam

Ingredients:

- 4 cups ripe cantaloupe, peeled, seeded, and diced
- 2 cups granulated sugar
- Juice of 1 lemon
- 1 vanilla bean, split and seeds scraped (or 2 teaspoons pure vanilla extract)

Instructions:

In a large, heavy-bottomed saucepan, combine the diced cantaloupe and granulated sugar. Stir well to coat the cantaloupe in sugar and let it sit for about 1 hour to allow the flavors to meld.

After the resting period, add the lemon juice to the saucepan and stir to combine.

Place the saucepan over medium heat, bringing the cantaloupe mixture to a boil. Once boiling, reduce the heat to low and let it simmer, stirring occasionally.

Continue simmering the jam until the cantaloupe softens and the mixture thickens, usually around 25-30 minutes.

If using a vanilla bean, add the scraped seeds and the split vanilla bean to the pot. If using vanilla extract, add it later in the process.

To test for doneness, place a small amount of the jam on a chilled plate. If it forms a gel-like consistency, it's ready.

Remove the saucepan from heat and let the cantaloupe and vanilla jam cool for a few minutes.

Spoon the jam into sterilized jars, leaving about 1/4-inch headspace. Wipe the jar rims with a clean, damp cloth to ensure a proper seal.

Seal the jars with sterilized lids and tighten the bands. Process the jars in a water bath for long-term storage or store them in the refrigerator for short-term use.

Spread this unique cantaloupe and vanilla jam on toast, use it in desserts, or pair it with cheese for a delightful combination of flavors!

Caramel Apple Jam

Ingredients:

- 6 cups apples, peeled, cored, and finely chopped (use a mix of sweet and tart apples)
- 2 cups granulated sugar
- 1 cup brown sugar
- 1/2 cup apple cider vinegar
- 1 teaspoon ground cinnamon
- 1/4 teaspoon ground nutmeg
- 1/4 teaspoon salt
- 1 cup caramel sauce (store-bought or homemade)
- 1/4 cup lemon juice

Instructions:

In a large, heavy-bottomed saucepan, combine the finely chopped apples, granulated sugar, brown sugar, apple cider vinegar, ground cinnamon, ground nutmeg, and salt. Stir well to combine.

Place the saucepan over medium heat, stirring to dissolve the sugars. Bring the mixture to a boil, then reduce the heat to low.

Simmer the apple mixture until the apples are soft and the mixture has thickened, usually around 25-30 minutes.

While simmering, prepare the caramel sauce if using homemade. Add the caramel sauce to the apple mixture, stirring to incorporate.

Add the lemon juice to the pot and continue simmering until the jam reaches the desired consistency.

To test for doneness, place a small amount of the jam on a chilled plate. If it forms a gel-like consistency, it's ready.

Remove the saucepan from heat and let the caramel apple jam cool for a few minutes. Spoon the jam into sterilized jars, leaving about 1/4-inch headspace. Wipe the jar rims with a clean, damp cloth to ensure a proper seal.

Seal the jars with sterilized lids and tighten the bands. Process the jars in a water bath for long-term storage or store them in the refrigerator for short-term use.

Spread this decadent caramel apple jam on toast, use it as a filling for pastries, or enjoy it as a topping for desserts and ice cream. The combination of sweet apples and rich caramel creates a delightful treat!

Honey Plum Jam

Ingredients:

- 4 cups ripe plums, pitted and chopped
- 1 cup honey
- 1/4 cup fresh lemon juice
- 1 teaspoon lemon zest

Instructions:

In a large, heavy-bottomed saucepan, combine the chopped plums, honey, fresh lemon juice, and lemon zest. Stir well to combine.

Place the saucepan over medium heat, bringing the plum mixture to a boil. Once boiling, reduce the heat to low and let it simmer, stirring occasionally.

Simmer the jam until the plums have softened, and the mixture has thickened, usually around 25-30 minutes.

To test for doneness, place a small amount of the jam on a chilled plate. If it forms a gel-like consistency, it's ready.

Remove the saucepan from heat and let the honey plum jam cool for a few minutes.

Spoon the jam into sterilized jars, leaving about 1/4-inch headspace. Wipe the jar rims with a clean, damp cloth to ensure a proper seal.

Seal the jars with sterilized lids and tighten the bands. Process the jars in a water bath for long-term storage or store them in the refrigerator for short-term use.

Spread this delightful honey plum jam on warm scones, toast, or use it as a glaze for meats. The combination of sweet plums and the natural sweetness of honey creates a rich and flavorful jam!

Pomegranate Raspberry Jam

Ingredients:

- 2 cups fresh raspberries
- 2 cups pomegranate arils (seeds)
- 3 cups granulated sugar
- 1/4 cup fresh lemon juice
- 1 tablespoon pomegranate molasses (optional)

Instructions:

In a large, heavy-bottomed saucepan, combine the fresh raspberries, pomegranate arils, granulated sugar, and fresh lemon juice. Stir well to combine. Place the saucepan over medium heat, stirring to dissolve the sugar. Bring the mixture to a boil, then reduce the heat to low.

Simmer the jam, stirring occasionally, until the raspberries break down, and the mixture thickens. This usually takes about 20-25 minutes.

While simmering, skim off any foam that rises to the surface.

If using pomegranate molasses, add it to the jam and stir to incorporate. Pomegranate molasses adds depth and enhances the pomegranate flavor.

To test for doneness, place a small amount of the jam on a chilled plate. If it forms a gel-like consistency, it's ready.

Remove the saucepan from heat and let the pomegranate raspberry jam cool for a few minutes.

Spoon the jam into sterilized jars, leaving about 1/4-inch headspace. Wipe the jar rims with a clean, damp cloth to ensure a proper seal.

Seal the jars with sterilized lids and tighten the bands. Process the jars in a water bath for long-term storage or store them in the refrigerator for short-term use.

Spread this vibrant pomegranate raspberry jam on toast, use it as a topping for desserts, or incorporate it into your favorite recipes. The combination of tart raspberries and sweet pomegranate creates a deliciously balanced jam!

Peach Lavender Jam

Ingredients:

- 4 cups ripe peaches, peeled, pitted, and chopped
- 2 cups granulated sugar
- 1/4 cup fresh lemon juice
- 2 tablespoons culinary lavender buds

Instructions:

In a large, heavy-bottomed saucepan, combine the chopped peaches and granulated sugar. Stir well to coat the peaches in sugar and let them sit for about 1 hour to allow the flavors to meld.

After the resting period, add the fresh lemon juice to the saucepan and stir to combine.

Place the saucepan over medium heat, bringing the peach mixture to a boil. Once boiling, reduce the heat to low and let it simmer, stirring occasionally.

Simmer the peach mixture until the peaches are soft, and the mixture has thickened, usually around 25-30 minutes.

While simmering, add the culinary lavender buds to the pot, stirring to evenly distribute them in the mixture.

To test for doneness, place a small amount of the jam on a chilled plate. If it forms a gel-like consistency, it's ready.

Remove the saucepan from heat and let the peach lavender jam cool for a few minutes.

Spoon the jam into sterilized jars, leaving about 1/4-inch headspace. Wipe the jar rims with a clean, damp cloth to ensure a proper seal.

Seal the jars with sterilized lids and tighten the bands. Process the jars in a water bath for long-term storage or store them in the refrigerator for short-term use.

Spread this fragrant peach lavender jam on warm scones, toast, or use it as a filling for pastries.

The combination of sweet peaches and aromatic lavender creates a delightful and sophisticated flavor!

Blueberry Basil Jam

Ingredients:

- 4 cups fresh blueberries
- 2 cups granulated sugar
- 1/4 cup fresh lemon juice
- 1/4 cup fresh basil, finely chopped

Instructions:

In a large, heavy-bottomed saucepan, combine the fresh blueberries and granulated sugar. Stir well to coat the blueberries in sugar and let them sit for about 1 hour to allow the flavors to meld.
After the resting period, add the fresh lemon juice to the saucepan and stir to combine.
Place the saucepan over medium heat, bringing the blueberry mixture to a boil. Once boiling, reduce the heat to low and let it simmer, stirring occasionally.
Simmer the blueberry mixture until the blueberries break down, and the mixture has thickened, usually around 20-25 minutes.
While simmering, add the finely chopped fresh basil to the pot, stirring to evenly distribute it in the mixture.
To test for doneness, place a small amount of the jam on a chilled plate. If it forms a gel-like consistency, it's ready.
Remove the saucepan from heat and let the blueberry basil jam cool for a few minutes.
Spoon the jam into sterilized jars, leaving about 1/4-inch headspace. Wipe the jar rims with a clean, damp cloth to ensure a proper seal.
Seal the jars with sterilized lids and tighten the bands. Process the jars in a water bath for long-term storage or store them in the refrigerator for short-term use.

Spread this unique blueberry basil jam on toast, use it as a topping for desserts, or pair it with cheese for a delightful burst of flavors!

Cherry Port Wine Jam

Ingredients:

- 4 cups fresh cherries, pitted and halved
- 2 cups granulated sugar
- 1/2 cup ruby port wine
- 2 tablespoons lemon juice
- 1 teaspoon lemon zest

Instructions:

> In a large, heavy-bottomed saucepan, combine the pitted and halved fresh cherries with granulated sugar. Stir well to coat the cherries in sugar and let them sit for about 1 hour to allow the flavors to meld.
> After the resting period, add the ruby port wine to the saucepan and stir to combine.
> Place the saucepan over medium heat, bringing the cherry mixture to a boil. Once boiling, reduce the heat to low and let it simmer, stirring occasionally.
> Simmer the cherry mixture until the cherries are softened, and the mixture has thickened, usually around 25-30 minutes.
> While simmering, add the lemon juice and lemon zest to the pot, stirring to incorporate.
> To test for doneness, place a small amount of the jam on a chilled plate. If it forms a gel-like consistency, it's ready.
> Remove the saucepan from heat and let the cherry port wine jam cool for a few minutes.
> Spoon the jam into sterilized jars, leaving about 1/4-inch headspace. Wipe the jar rims with a clean, damp cloth to ensure a proper seal.
> Seal the jars with sterilized lids and tighten the bands. Process the jars in a water bath for long-term storage or store them in the refrigerator for short-term use.

Spread this luxurious cherry port wine jam on crusty bread, use it as an accompaniment for cheese, or incorporate it into desserts for a touch of sophistication!

Watermelon Mint Jam

Ingredients:

- 4 cups seedless watermelon, finely chopped
- 2 cups granulated sugar
- 1/4 cup fresh lemon juice
- 2 tablespoons fresh mint, finely chopped

Instructions:

In a large, heavy-bottomed saucepan, combine the finely chopped seedless watermelon and granulated sugar. Stir well to combine and let it sit for about 1 hour to allow the flavors to meld.

After the resting period, add the fresh lemon juice to the saucepan and stir to combine.

Place the saucepan over medium heat, bringing the watermelon mixture to a boil. Once boiling, reduce the heat to low and let it simmer, stirring occasionally.

Simmer the watermelon mixture until it thickens and reaches a jam-like consistency, usually around 20-25 minutes.

While simmering, add the finely chopped fresh mint to the pot, stirring to evenly distribute it in the mixture.

To test for doneness, place a small amount of the jam on a chilled plate. If it forms a gel-like consistency, it's ready.

Remove the saucepan from heat and let the watermelon mint jam cool for a few minutes.

Spoon the jam into sterilized jars, leaving about 1/4-inch headspace. Wipe the jar rims with a clean, damp cloth to ensure a proper seal.

Seal the jars with sterilized lids and tighten the bands. Process the jars in a water bath for long-term storage or store them in the refrigerator for short-term use.

Spread this refreshing watermelon mint jam on toast, use it as a topping for desserts, or add a spoonful to your favorite beverages for a burst of summer flavor!

Guava Passionfruit Jam

Ingredients:

- 4 cups guava, peeled, seeded, and mashed
- 2 cups passionfruit pulp (about 10-12 passionfruits)
- 3 cups granulated sugar
- 1/4 cup fresh lime juice

Instructions:

In a large, heavy-bottomed saucepan, combine the mashed guava and passionfruit pulp. Stir well to combine.

Place the saucepan over medium heat, stirring to dissolve the sugar. Bring the mixture to a boil, then reduce the heat to low.

Simmer the jam, stirring occasionally, until it thickens and reaches a jam-like consistency, usually around 25-30 minutes.

While simmering, add the fresh lime juice to the pot, stirring to incorporate.

To test for doneness, place a small amount of the jam on a chilled plate. If it forms a gel-like consistency, it's ready.

Remove the saucepan from heat and let the guava passionfruit jam cool for a few minutes.

Spoon the jam into sterilized jars, leaving about 1/4-inch headspace. Wipe the jar rims with a clean, damp cloth to ensure a proper seal.

Seal the jars with sterilized lids and tighten the bands. Process the jars in a water bath for long-term storage or store them in the refrigerator for short-term use.

Spread this tropical guava passionfruit jam on toast, use it as a topping for yogurt, or incorporate it into desserts for a burst of exotic flavors!

Pumpkin Spice Jam

Ingredients:

- 4 cups canned pumpkin puree
- 2 cups granulated sugar
- 1 cup brown sugar
- 1/2 cup apple cider
- 1 tablespoon lemon juice
- 1 teaspoon ground cinnamon
- 1/2 teaspoon ground nutmeg
- 1/4 teaspoon ground cloves
- 1/4 teaspoon ground ginger
- Pinch of salt

Instructions:

In a large, heavy-bottomed saucepan, combine the canned pumpkin puree, granulated sugar, brown sugar, apple cider, and lemon juice. Stir well to combine.

Place the saucepan over medium heat, stirring to dissolve the sugars. Bring the mixture to a boil, then reduce the heat to low.

Simmer the pumpkin mixture, stirring occasionally, until it thickens and reaches a jam-like consistency, usually around 25-30 minutes.

While simmering, add the ground cinnamon, ground nutmeg, ground cloves, ground ginger, and a pinch of salt to the pot. Stir to incorporate the spices evenly.

Taste the jam and adjust the spices or sweetness according to your preference by adding more sugar or spices if needed.

To test for doneness, place a small amount of the jam on a chilled plate. If it forms a gel-like consistency, it's ready.

Remove the saucepan from heat and let the pumpkin spice jam cool for a few minutes.

Spoon the jam into sterilized jars, leaving about 1/4-inch headspace. Wipe the jar rims with a clean, damp cloth to ensure a proper seal.

Seal the jars with sterilized lids and tighten the bands. Process the jars in a water bath for long-term storage or store them in the refrigerator for short-term use.

Spread this comforting pumpkin spice jam on toast, muffins, or use it as a filling for pastries.

The combination of pumpkin and warm spices creates a delightful fall-flavored treat!

Rhubarb Ginger Jam

Ingredients:

- 4 cups rhubarb, diced
- 2 cups granulated sugar
- 1/4 cup fresh lemon juice
- 2 tablespoons fresh ginger, grated
- Zest of 1 lemon

Instructions:

In a large, heavy-bottomed saucepan, combine the diced rhubarb and granulated sugar. Stir well to coat the rhubarb in sugar and let it sit for about 1 hour to allow the flavors to meld.

After the resting period, add the fresh lemon juice to the saucepan and stir to combine.

Place the saucepan over medium heat, bringing the rhubarb mixture to a boil. Once boiling, reduce the heat to low and let it simmer, stirring occasionally.

Simmer the rhubarb mixture until the rhubarb is soft, and the mixture has thickened, usually around 20-25 minutes.

While simmering, add the grated fresh ginger and lemon zest to the pot, stirring to evenly distribute them in the mixture.

To test for doneness, place a small amount of the jam on a chilled plate. If it forms a gel-like consistency, it's ready.

Remove the saucepan from heat and let the rhubarb ginger jam cool for a few minutes.

Spoon the jam into sterilized jars, leaving about 1/4-inch headspace. Wipe the jar rims with a clean, damp cloth to ensure a proper seal.

Seal the jars with sterilized lids and tighten the bands. Process the jars in a water bath for long-term storage or store them in the refrigerator for short-term use.

Spread this delightful rhubarb ginger jam on toast, scones, or use it as a tangy accompaniment for cheese and crackers. The combination of tart rhubarb and spicy ginger creates a unique and flavorful jam!

Banana Jam

Ingredients:

- 4 cups ripe bananas, mashed (about 6-8 bananas)
- 2 cups granulated sugar
- 1/4 cup fresh lemon juice
- 1 teaspoon ground cinnamon
- 1/4 teaspoon ground nutmeg
- Pinch of salt

Instructions:

In a large, heavy-bottomed saucepan, combine the mashed ripe bananas and granulated sugar. Stir well to combine.

Place the saucepan over medium heat, stirring to dissolve the sugar. Bring the mixture to a boil, then reduce the heat to low.

Simmer the banana mixture, stirring occasionally, until it thickens and reaches a jam-like consistency, usually around 20-25 minutes.

While simmering, add the fresh lemon juice, ground cinnamon, ground nutmeg, and a pinch of salt to the pot. Stir to incorporate the spices evenly.

Taste the jam and adjust the spices or sweetness according to your preference by adding more sugar or spices if needed.

To test for doneness, place a small amount of the jam on a chilled plate. If it forms a gel-like consistency, it's ready.

Remove the saucepan from heat and let the banana jam cool for a few minutes.

Spoon the jam into sterilized jars, leaving about 1/4-inch headspace. Wipe the jar rims with a clean, damp cloth to ensure a proper seal.

Seal the jars with sterilized lids and tighten the bands. Process the jars in a water bath for long-term storage or store them in the refrigerator for short-term use.

Spread this sweet and spiced banana jam on toast, pancakes, or use it as a filling for pastries. The natural sweetness of bananas combined with cinnamon and nutmeg creates a deliciously comforting jam!

Cucumber Dill Jam

Ingredients:

- 4 cups cucumbers, peeled, seeded, and finely chopped
- 2 cups granulated sugar

- 1/4 cup fresh lemon juice
- 2 tablespoons fresh dill, finely chopped
- 1 teaspoon mustard seeds
- 1/4 teaspoon celery seeds
- Pinch of salt

Instructions:

In a large, heavy-bottomed saucepan, combine the finely chopped cucumbers and granulated sugar. Stir well to combine.

Place the saucepan over medium heat, stirring to dissolve the sugar. Bring the mixture to a boil, then reduce the heat to low.

Simmer the cucumber mixture, stirring occasionally, until it thickens and reaches a jam-like consistency, usually around 25-30 minutes.

While simmering, add the fresh lemon juice, finely chopped fresh dill, mustard seeds, celery seeds, and a pinch of salt to the pot. Stir to incorporate the flavors evenly.

Taste the jam and adjust the salt or dill according to your preference.

To test for doneness, place a small amount of the jam on a chilled plate. If it forms a gel-like consistency, it's ready.

Remove the saucepan from heat and let the cucumber dill jam cool for a few minutes.

Spoon the jam into sterilized jars, leaving about 1/4-inch headspace. Wipe the jar rims with a clean, damp cloth to ensure a proper seal.

Seal the jars with sterilized lids and tighten the bands. Process the jars in a water bath for long-term storage or store them in the refrigerator for short-term use.

Spread this refreshing cucumber dill jam on crackers, use it as a condiment for sandwiches, or enjoy it as a unique topping for grilled meats and seafood!

Tomato Basil Jam

Ingredients:

- 4 cups ripe tomatoes, peeled, seeded, and chopped
- 2 cups granulated sugar
- 1/4 cup fresh lemon juice
- 2 tablespoons fresh basil, finely chopped
- 1 teaspoon balsamic vinegar
- 1/4 teaspoon red pepper flakes (optional)
- Pinch of salt

Instructions:

In a large, heavy-bottomed saucepan, combine the peeled, seeded, and chopped tomatoes with granulated sugar. Stir well to combine.

Place the saucepan over medium heat, stirring to dissolve the sugar. Bring the mixture to a boil, then reduce the heat to low.

Simmer the tomato mixture, stirring occasionally, until it thickens and reaches a jam-like consistency, usually around 25-30 minutes.

While simmering, add the fresh lemon juice, finely chopped fresh basil, balsamic vinegar, red pepper flakes (if using), and a pinch of salt to the pot. Stir to incorporate the flavors evenly.

Taste the jam and adjust the salt or red pepper flakes according to your preference.

To test for doneness, place a small amount of the jam on a chilled plate. If it forms a gel-like consistency, it's ready.

Remove the saucepan from heat and let the tomato basil jam cool for a few minutes.

Spoon the jam into sterilized jars, leaving about 1/4-inch headspace. Wipe the jar rims with a clean, damp cloth to ensure a proper seal.

Seal the jars with sterilized lids and tighten the bands. Process the jars in a water bath for long-term storage or store them in the refrigerator for short-term use.

Spread this savory tomato basil jam on crusty bread, use it as a condiment for burgers, or incorporate it into appetizers for a burst of fresh and herby flavor!

Elderberry Orange Jam

Ingredients:

- 4 cups elderberries, stems removed
- 2 cups granulated sugar
- Zest and juice of 2 oranges
- 1 tablespoon fresh lemon juice
- 1/2 teaspoon ground cinnamon
- 1/4 teaspoon ground cloves

Instructions:

In a large, heavy-bottomed saucepan, combine the elderberries and granulated sugar. Stir well to combine.

Place the saucepan over medium heat, stirring to dissolve the sugar. Bring the mixture to a boil, then reduce the heat to low.

Simmer the elderberry mixture, stirring occasionally, until the berries soften and the mixture thickens, usually around 20-25 minutes.

While simmering, add the zest and juice of 2 oranges, fresh lemon juice, ground cinnamon, and ground cloves to the pot. Stir to incorporate the flavors evenly.

Continue simmering the jam until it reaches a jam-like consistency, and the flavors meld together.

To test for doneness, place a small amount of the jam on a chilled plate. If it forms a gel-like consistency, it's ready.

Remove the saucepan from heat and let the elderberry orange jam cool for a few minutes.

Spoon the jam into sterilized jars, leaving about 1/4-inch headspace. Wipe the jar rims with a clean, damp cloth to ensure a proper seal.

Seal the jars with sterilized lids and tighten the bands. Process the jars in a water bath for long-term storage or store them in the refrigerator for short-term use.

Spread this rich and flavorful elderberry orange jam on toast, use it as a topping for desserts, or pair it with cheese for a delightful combination of sweet and citrusy notes!

Chocolate Raspberry Jam

Ingredients:

- 4 cups fresh raspberries
- 2 cups granulated sugar
- 1/4 cup cocoa powder
- 1/4 cup dark chocolate, finely chopped
- 2 tablespoons fresh lemon juice
- 1 teaspoon vanilla extract

Instructions:

In a large, heavy-bottomed saucepan, combine the fresh raspberries and granulated sugar. Stir well to combine.

Place the saucepan over medium heat, stirring to dissolve the sugar. Bring the mixture to a boil, then reduce the heat to low.

Simmer the raspberry mixture, stirring occasionally, until the berries break down and the mixture thickens, usually around 20-25 minutes.

While simmering, add the cocoa powder and finely chopped dark chocolate to the pot. Stir continuously to ensure the chocolate is fully melted and incorporated into the jam.

Add the fresh lemon juice and vanilla extract to the pot, stirring to enhance the flavors.

Continue simmering the jam until it reaches a thick, spreadable consistency.

To test for doneness, place a small amount of the jam on a chilled plate. If it forms a gel-like consistency, it's ready.

Remove the saucepan from heat and let the chocolate raspberry jam cool for a few minutes.

Spoon the jam into sterilized jars, leaving about 1/4-inch headspace. Wipe the jar rims with a clean, damp cloth to ensure a proper seal.

Seal the jars with sterilized lids and tighten the bands. Process the jars in a water bath for long-term storage or store them in the refrigerator for short-term use.

Spread this indulgent chocolate raspberry jam on bread, muffins, or use it as a decadent filling for pastries. The combination of rich chocolate and sweet raspberries creates a delightful treat!

Lemon Thyme Jam

Ingredients:

- 4 cups fresh lemons, peeled, seeded, and finely chopped
- 2 cups granulated sugar
- Zest of 2 lemons
- 2 tablespoons fresh thyme leaves, finely chopped
- 1/4 cup fresh lemon juice

Instructions:

In a large, heavy-bottomed saucepan, combine the finely chopped fresh lemons and granulated sugar. Stir well to combine.

Place the saucepan over medium heat, stirring to dissolve the sugar. Bring the mixture to a boil, then reduce the heat to low.

Simmer the lemon mixture, stirring occasionally, until the lemons break down and the mixture thickens, usually around 20-25 minutes.

While simmering, add the lemon zest and finely chopped fresh thyme leaves to the pot. Stir to incorporate the flavors evenly.

Pour in the fresh lemon juice, stirring to enhance the citrusy notes.

Continue simmering the jam until it reaches a thick, spreadable consistency.

To test for doneness, place a small amount of the jam on a chilled plate. If it forms a gel-like consistency, it's ready.

Remove the saucepan from heat and let the lemon thyme jam cool for a few minutes.

Spoon the jam into sterilized jars, leaving about 1/4-inch headspace. Wipe the jar rims with a clean, damp cloth to ensure a proper seal.

Seal the jars with sterilized lids and tighten the bands. Process the jars in a water bath for long-term storage or store them in the refrigerator for short-term use.

Spread this vibrant lemon thyme jam on toast, scones, or use it as a zesty accompaniment for cheeses and grilled meats. The combination of citrusy lemons and aromatic thyme creates a refreshing and herbaceous flavor!

Kiwi Strawberry Jam

Ingredients:

- 4 cups ripe kiwi, peeled and diced
- 2 cups fresh strawberries, hulled and chopped
- 3 cups granulated sugar

- 1/4 cup fresh lemon juice
- 1 teaspoon lemon zest

Instructions:

In a large, heavy-bottomed saucepan, combine the diced kiwi, chopped strawberries, and granulated sugar. Stir well to combine.

Place the saucepan over medium heat, stirring to dissolve the sugar. Bring the mixture to a boil, then reduce the heat to low.

Simmer the kiwi and strawberry mixture, stirring occasionally, until the fruits soften, and the mixture thickens, usually around 20-25 minutes.

While simmering, add the fresh lemon juice and lemon zest to the pot. Stir to incorporate the citrusy flavors.

Continue simmering the jam until it reaches a thick, spreadable consistency.

To test for doneness, place a small amount of the jam on a chilled plate. If it forms a gel-like consistency, it's ready.

Remove the saucepan from heat and let the kiwi strawberry jam cool for a few minutes.

Spoon the jam into sterilized jars, leaving about 1/4-inch headspace. Wipe the jar rims with a clean, damp cloth to ensure a proper seal.

Seal the jars with sterilized lids and tighten the bands. Process the jars in a water bath for long-term storage or store them in the refrigerator for short-term use.

Spread this delightful kiwi strawberry jam on toast, pancakes, or use it as a topping for desserts.

The combination of sweet strawberries and tangy kiwi creates a deliciously fruity jam!

Vanilla Peach Jam

Ingredients:

- 4 cups ripe peaches, peeled, pitted, and chopped
- 2 cups granulated sugar
- 1/4 cup fresh lemon juice
- 1 vanilla bean, split and seeds scraped (or 1 tablespoon vanilla extract)

Instructions:

> In a large, heavy-bottomed saucepan, combine the chopped peaches and granulated sugar. Stir well to coat the peaches in sugar and let them sit for about 1 hour to allow the flavors to meld.
>
> After the resting period, add the fresh lemon juice to the saucepan and stir to combine.
>
> Place the saucepan over medium heat, bringing the peach mixture to a boil. Once boiling, reduce the heat to low and let it simmer, stirring occasionally.
>
> Simmer the peach mixture until the peaches are soft, and the mixture has thickened, usually around 20-25 minutes.
>
> While simmering, add the scraped seeds of the vanilla bean (or vanilla extract) to the pot, stirring to evenly distribute the vanilla flavor.
>
> To test for doneness, place a small amount of the jam on a chilled plate. If it forms a gel-like consistency, it's ready.
>
> Remove the saucepan from heat and let the vanilla peach jam cool for a few minutes.
>
> Spoon the jam into sterilized jars, leaving about 1/4-inch headspace. Wipe the jar rims with a clean, damp cloth to ensure a proper seal.
>
> Seal the jars with sterilized lids and tighten the bands. Process the jars in a water bath for long-term storage or store them in the refrigerator for short-term use.

Spread this vanilla-infused peach jam on toast, use it as a filling for pastries, or swirl it into yogurt for a delightful treat. The combination of sweet peaches and aromatic vanilla creates a heavenly flavor!

Minted Melon Jam

Ingredients:

- 4 cups ripe melon (cantaloupe or honeydew), peeled, seeded, and finely chopped
- 2 cups granulated sugar
- 1/4 cup fresh lemon juice
- 2 tablespoons fresh mint, finely chopped

Instructions:

In a large, heavy-bottomed saucepan, combine the finely chopped melon and granulated sugar. Stir well to combine.

Place the saucepan over medium heat, stirring to dissolve the sugar. Bring the mixture to a boil, then reduce the heat to low.

Simmer the melon mixture, stirring occasionally, until the melon softens, and the mixture thickens, usually around 20-25 minutes.

While simmering, add the fresh lemon juice and finely chopped fresh mint to the pot. Stir to incorporate the minty freshness.

Continue simmering the jam until it reaches a thick, spreadable consistency.

To test for doneness, place a small amount of the jam on a chilled plate. If it forms a gel-like consistency, it's ready.

Remove the saucepan from heat and let the minted melon jam cool for a few minutes.

Spoon the jam into sterilized jars, leaving about 1/4-inch headspace. Wipe the jar rims with a clean, damp cloth to ensure a proper seal.

Seal the jars with sterilized lids and tighten the bands. Process the jars in a water bath for long-term storage or store them in the refrigerator for short-term use.

Spread this refreshing minted melon jam on toast, use it as a topping for desserts, or mix it into yogurt for a cool and delightful twist. The combination of sweet melon and mint creates a burst of summery flavor!

Gingerbread Apple Jam

Ingredients:

- 4 cups apples, peeled, cored, and finely chopped
- 2 cups brown sugar
- 1/4 cup fresh lemon juice
- 1 teaspoon ground cinnamon
- 1/2 teaspoon ground ginger

- 1/4 teaspoon ground cloves
- 1/4 teaspoon ground nutmeg
- Pinch of salt
- 1/4 cup molasses

Instructions:

In a large, heavy-bottomed saucepan, combine the finely chopped apples and brown sugar. Stir well to combine.

Place the saucepan over medium heat, stirring to dissolve the sugar. Bring the mixture to a boil, then reduce the heat to low.

Simmer the apple mixture, stirring occasionally, until the apples are soft, and the mixture has thickened, usually around 20-25 minutes.

While simmering, add the fresh lemon juice, ground cinnamon, ground ginger, ground cloves, ground nutmeg, and a pinch of salt to the pot. Stir to incorporate the warm spices.

Pour in the molasses, stirring to enhance the gingerbread flavor.

Continue simmering the jam until it reaches a thick, spreadable consistency.

To test for doneness, place a small amount of the jam on a chilled plate. If it forms a gel-like consistency, it's ready.

Remove the saucepan from heat and let the gingerbread apple jam cool for a few minutes.

Spoon the jam into sterilized jars, leaving about 1/4-inch headspace. Wipe the jar rims with a clean, damp cloth to ensure a proper seal.

Seal the jars with sterilized lids and tighten the bands. Process the jars in a water bath for long-term storage or store them in the refrigerator for short-term use.

Spread this delightful gingerbread apple jam on toast, muffins, or use it as a filling for holiday-inspired pastries. The combination of spiced apples and molasses creates a warm and comforting flavor!